BOOK ANALYSIS

By Isabelle Bousquette

Tender is the Night
BY F. SCOTT FITZGERALD

F. SCOTT FITZGERALD

AMERICAN NOVELIST AND SHORT STORY WRITER

- **Born in St. Paul, Minnesota in 1896.**
- **Died in Hollywood, California in 1940.**
- **Notable works:**
  - *This Side of Paradise* (1920), novel
  - *The Beautiful and Damned* (1922), novel
  - *The Great Gatsby* (1925), novel

Francis Scott Fitzgerald was an American writer most famous for his touching and often tragic depictions of the Jazz Age. After attending a boys' school in Minnesota, Fitzgerald found his way to Princeton, where he became occupied with attaining social status. He spent time writing about the spirit of America, interested in both its romance and its vulgarity. Ultimately, Fitzgerald left Princeton to fight in the First World War.

In 1920, Fitzgerald published *This Side of Paradise*, a semi-autobiographical novel that made him famous on the literary scene. Fitzgerald moved with his family to France, joining a group of American literary and artistic expatriates that had become disillusioned with their country. This group, which included Ernest Hemingway (American novelist, 1899-1961) and Gertrude Stein (American novelist, 1974-1946), became known as the Lost Generation. In 1925, Fitzgerald published his most famous novel, *The Great Gatsby*, which stood as a testament to the futility of the American dream.

TENDER IS THE NIGHT

A DISILLUSIONED ROMANCE

- **Genre:** novel
- **Reference edition:** Fitzgerald, F. S. (2000) *Tender is the Night*. London: Penguin Books Ltd.
- **1st edition:** 1934
- **Themes:** mental health, marriage, love, affairs, youth, social status, money

Tender is the Night was published in 1934, a full nine years after Fitzgerald's greatest success, *The Great Gatsby*. In the intervening years, Fitzgerald and his wife, Zelda, had moved to Europe to escape the widespread disillusionment felt in America in the wake of World War I. Their relationship had deteriorated by the 1930s, partially owing to Zelda's declining mental health. Zelda had been affected by bouts of mental illness and spent time in various health clinics and sanatoriums during the early 1930s. The emotional stress of Zelda's illness coupled with the financial stress of her medical bills were undoubtedly contributing factors to Fitzgerald's lack of writing in these years. Fitzgerald eventually finished *Tender is the Night*, but the book met with little commercial success, especially in comparison to *The Great Gatsby*.

It is easy to see how Fitzgerald's love for Zelda and the tragedy of her deteriorating mental health contributed to his inventions of Dick and Nicole Diver, the protagonists of *Tender is the Night*. Dick is a renowned psychiatrist who falls in love with and marries one of his patients. The pressure felt by Fitzgerald as a caregiver for his wife naturally manifests itself in the presentation of Dick and Nicole's doctor/patient/lover relationship. However, Fitzgerald is said to have based the specifics of Dick and Nicole on his friends Gerald and Sara Murphy (American expatriates, 1888-1964 and 1883-1975, respectively).

The novel is divided into three parts. Interestingly, a portion of the second part takes place chronologically before the first part. In 1951, a revised version of the novel was published which claimed to be part of a reorganisation project by Fitzgerald himself in which he considered placing the events in chronological order. However, scholarly opinion has come to believe that Fitzgerald abandoned the reordering project in favour of the original edition. The description of the early days of Dick and Nicole's romance is thus marked with a tragic tinge when we already know from the beginning of the novel that Dick ends up having an affair.

SUMMARY

DICK AND ROSEMARY

Rosemary Hoyt, a star of American film, is travelling in the French Riviera with her mother, Elsie Spiers, when she meets Dick and Nicole Diver. The Divers are a beautiful couple with two children summering in the Riviera with a group of friends.

Rosemary is immediately attracted to Dick and tells her mother she is in love with him. She admires Nicole as well, but Nicole senses Rosemary's affection for Dick. Nevertheless, the Divers invite Rosemary into their inner circle. At a dinner party to which Rosemary is invited, Violet McKisco, a friend of the Divers, claims to have witnessed a shocking moment in the bathroom. Another friend, Tommy Barban, insists that Violet say no more. The misunderstanding ultimately leads to a duel between Tommy and Violet's husband, but nobody is injured in the drunken brawl.

Rosemary travels to Paris with the Divers, where she continues trying to win Dick's affection. Dick feels himself falling for Rosemary, but his love for Nicole is so strong that he knows he cannot betray her. On Rosemary's 18th birthday, she has her first sip of champagne. In her tipsiness, she clumsily tries to seduce Dick. He reasserts his commitment to Nicole, but not due to a lack of temptation.

In Paris, Dick's close friend Abe North gets into trouble in a bar and brings the troublemakers back to Dick's hotel. The altercation ends with a black man being murdered in Rosemary's hotel room. Dick calls the hotel manager and, in order to save Rosemary from a publicity scandal, brings her into his room. There they find Nicole sitting by the bathtub swaying and muttering incoherently. Rosemary believes that Violet McKisco must have witnessed a similar scene in the Riviera.

DICK AND NICOLE

In Part 2, we go back in time to meet a young 28-year-old Dick returning from fighting in World War I. While visiting his friend, Franz Gregarovius, Dick is reminded of a young female patient at Franz's clinic in Switzerland. This patient is Nicole, and she has been writing him letters since his last visit to the clinic.

Dick learns of Nicole's history. Her father, Devereux Warren, is from a wealthy family in Chicago. He is the one who dropped Nicole off at the clinic and, after questioning, admits that he sexually abused her when she was a child. Nicole has been diagnosed with schizophrenia, but has been coping with it much better in recent years. Her doctor tells Dick to break off his childish flirtation with her. However, Dick instead decides to marry her. Nicole's sister, Baby Warren, is somewhat suspicious of the match because Nicole is far wealthier than Dick, but ultimately agrees to it.

Dick and Nicole marry, but after the birth of their second child, she falls into occasional relapses. They spend time in the Riviera (where we catch up with the beginning of the narrative) and the Swiss Alps. There, Dick runs into Franz, who proposes that the two of them open up a clinic together. At Nicole's suggestion, Dick agrees and the clinic becomes a reality.

As Dick begins drinking more and more, troubles in his marriage arise. Nicole fears that he is cheating on her with his patients. Her agitation leads her to crash their car. After this incident, Dick decides to travel on his own for a while. On his travels, he learns that his father has passed away in America. He also learns that his friend Abe North has died. Lonely and depressed, Dick meets Rosemary in Rome. They consummate their affair, but he soon ends the romance. After an excessive night of drinking, he ends up in a brawl with some local cab drivers that lands him in Italian jail. Nicole's sister, Baby, who also happens to be in Rome, bails him out.

DICK WITHOUT NICOLE

When Dick returns to the clinic, he is drinking more and more. Franz is aware of this and considers how he might convince Dick to leave the venture. He sends Dick on a house call where Dick overhears that Nicole's father has been taken ill in America. Mr. Warren has requested to see Nicole in order to make amends. Nicole, when she hears of this, desires to see him as well. However, before she can arrange the trip, her father simply walks out of his deathbed and disappears. Back at the clinic, a patient complains that he can constantly smell alcohol on Dick's breath. This is the perfect opportunity for Franz to ask his partner to leave the clinic. The decision to part ways is mutual and the Divers return to the Riviera.

Dick and Nicole's marriage continues to deteriorate, primarily owing to his alcoholic behaviour. He begins to offend various friends and the cook at their villa. Rosemary visits the Riviera. During her stay, Dick makes a fool out of himself trying to impress her. Nicole, finding Dick increasingly difficult to live with, decides to embark on an affair with Tommy Barban.

When Dick and Nicole go out together to get haircuts, Tommy finds them in the barber shop and demands that the three of them sit down together. He tells Dick that Nicole no longer loves him and that he should gracefully withdraw from the marriage. Dick is not surprised, but tells Tommy that he and Nicole will sort out the details in private.

Nicole later marries Tommy and Dick moves back to America to continue his psychology practice. The two intermittently keep in touch through letters and it seems Dick has moved from rural town to rural town in America. He has failed to put down real roots in a psychology practice or in a relationship.

CHARACTER STUDY

DICK DIVER

We are first introduced to Dick through the lens of Rosemary. Despite, or perhaps because of, his being somewhat older, she immediately admires him, both for his physique and for his stature. Fitzgerald describes Rosemary's infatuation with him:

> "His complexion was reddish and weather-burned, so was his short hair--a light growth of it rolled down his arms and hands. His eyes were of a bright, hard blue. His nose was somewhat pointed and there was never any doubt at whom he was looking or talking--and this is a flattering attention, for who looks at us?--glances fall upon us, curious or disinterested, nothing more. His voice, with some faint Irish melody running through it, wooed the world, yet she felt the layer of hardness in him, of self-control and of self-discipline, her own virtues." (p. 28)

He has a certain charm that makes everyone he talks to feel comfortable and valued. This means that he and Nicole are extremely popular figures amongst the American expatriates in Europe. They are constantly surrounded by friends and invited to glamorous parties.

As the novel progresses, we learn more about Dick's ambitions. He wants to be a great psychologist and publishes a series of psychological studies. His charming personality makes him a good psychologist; however, he often procrastinates and does not spend as much time writing as Nicole would like him to.

After Dick's marriage to Nicole, he is extremely conscious of their financial situation. Dick is of modest means, but Nicole's family is so rich as to be considered American royalty. Because of this, Nicole's sister, Baby Warren, feels that she has some control over Dick since the Warrens are financing his entire lifestyle. For this reason, when he is on his own, Dick tries not to spend any of Nicole's money. Still, the Warrens' money creates an odd power dynamic between Dick and Nicole.

As Dick gets older and begins drinking more and more, he loses his characteristic charm. At the beginning of the novel, he thrives in social environments and is a hit at every party; towards the end, he seems to offend people wherever he goes.

Dick's character follows a sharp downward trajectory. When we initially meet him from Rosemary's perspective, he is nothing short of god-like. When Nicole meets him, she is also entranced. However, his flaws become increasingly evident and he becomes rude, alcoholic and actually violent.

NICOLE WARREN DIVER

Nicole appears in the first part of the novel in the role of the jealous wife. Because we meet her from Rosemary's perspective, we initially see her as hard and unfriendly. Rosemary's first impression is that Nicole looks somewhat like a statue:

> "Her face could have been described in terms of conventional prettiness, but the effect was that it had been made first on the heroic scale with strong structure and marking, as if the features and vividness of brow and coloring, everything we associate with temperament and character had been molded with a Rodinesque intention, and then chiseled away in the direction of prettiness to a point where a single slip would have irreparably diminished its force and quality." (p. 25)

Rosemary views Nicole's prettiness as strong and hard. This is possibly a result of Rosemary's difficult past and upbringing. More likely, Rosemary views Nicole as hard and statuesque because Nicole senses Rosemary's feelings for Dick and thus is consciously distant.

In the second part of the book, we meet a very different version of Nicole. We learn that she was sexually abused by her father as a child and that as a result, she has been diagnosed with schizophrenia. However, after a few years in a clinic in Switzerland, she has mostly regained a competent mind and has blossomed into an attractive and charming young woman. Dick meets her there and, despite it being forbidden by her doctor, falls in love with her. Fitzgerald describes this version of Nicole:

> "Miss Warren emerged first in glimpses and then sharply when she saw him; as she crossed the threshold her face caught the room's last light and brought it outside with her. She walked to a rhythm--all that week there had been singing in her ears, summer songs of ardent skies and wild shade, and with his arrival the singing had become so loud she could have joined in with it." (p. 149)

This version of Nicole is sharply in contrast with her presentation at the beginning of the novel. Then, her beauty had been a result of statuesque hardness; here, it blooms and flows in conjunction with the natural world. Nicole's character displays a tension between unadulterated natural beauty and jealous fits of mental illness. Her extensive wealth means that she is financially independent, but her mental state means that she can never truly have that independence. As a former mental patient, she ultimately relies on Dick to take care of her. She strikes a blow for her own independence in her rash decision to begin an affair with Tommy Barban. However, we have the sense that she has simply swapped one caregiver for another.

ROSEMARY HOYT

In many ways, Rosemary is the central catalyst for the events of the novel. However, as it goes on, she becomes more of a device to drive a wedge between Dick and Nicole than a character in her own right. She is a beacon of youth and innocence, as implied by the title of her breakout film, "Daddy's Girl". Fitzgerald describes Rosemary as containing all the magic and charm of childhood:

"[She] had magic in her pink palms and her cheeks lit to a lovely flame, like the thrilling flush of children after their cold baths in the evening. Her fine forehead sloped gently up to where her hair, bordering it like an armorial shield, burst into lovelocks and waves and curlicues of ash blonde and gold. Her eyes were bright, big, clear, wet, and shining, the color of her cheeks was real, breaking close to the surface from the strong young pump of her heart. Her body hovered delicately on the last edge of childhood--she was almost eighteen, nearly complete, but the dew was still on her." (pp. 11-12)

As we view the first part of the novel from Rosemary's perspective, we find Dick handsome and enchanting and Nicole cold and distant. However, as the novel goes on and we discover the complex nuances of the Divers' marriage, we realise that Rosemary's perspective is intensely naive. She sees the world in simple terms, and those terms are often dictated by the advice of her mother. She falls for Dick, so she pursues Dick.

When Dick meets her later in Rome, she is a little older and a little less innocent. They finally consummate their affair, but she no longer represents for Dick what she used to: the charm of the unattainable. Once obtained, she no longer symbolises the perfection of youth and childlike innocence, and she quickly disappears from the narrative.

ANALYSIS

MENTAL HEALTH

Mental health is a driving force of many of the relationships in this novel. This is interesting because the novel was actually published at a historical moment when the collective emotional health of America seemed to be on the decline. After the trauma of World War I and the Great Depression, America was a changed nation. The novel itself speaks to this change in the American zeitgeist, calling the new America, "a society of veterans going to lay wreaths on the tombs of the dead... with a sort of swagger for a lost magnificence, a past effort, a forgotten sorrow." (p. 219).

Fitzgerald writes of an American spirit that has become lost and disillusioned due to past trauma. This trajectory is mirrored in the story of Nicole. She has endured a deeply disturbing past trauma which has forever affected her mental state. She stands for a whole group of Americans who lost some part of themselves or their minds during the difficult years behind them.

Mental health also functions in a less representational way within the world of the novel. Nicole's diagnosis is a true hardship, but it is also conquerable. It is a constant battle that must be fought, both by herself and by her husband, to find the better part of herself. Dick reflects on her illness, thinking:

> "A "schizophrêne" is well named as a split personality--Nicole was alternately a person to whom nothing need be explained and one to whom nothing could be explained...But the brilliance, the versatility of madness is akin to the resourcefulness of water seeping through, over and around a dike. It requires the united front of many people to work against it. He felt it necessary that this time Nicole cure herself; he wanted to wait until she remembered the other times, and revolted from them." (p. 210)

The fact that Nicole's illness is conquerable is perhaps the most tragic aspect of it. The responsibility often rests with Dick to make sure she is at ease and thus not prone to fits. Her fits occur when Dick shirks that responsibility and fails to hide his feelings for Rosemary. This blurred line between husband/wife and doctor/patient puts an increased strain on their relationship.

Nicole's mental illness makes her simultaneously one of the most sympathetic characters in the novel and one of the most dislikeable. She is a strong woman bearing the brunt of significant pain and trauma; however, she also becomes a grating professional responsibility for Dick. At the end of the novel, he begins to realise why her initial doctor had warned against his marrying her.

Nevertheless, at the end of the novel, Nicole steps out of an unhappy marriage and chooses to be with a new man who makes her happy. In the end, she seems to conquer her illness. Meanwhile, Dick becomes an alcoholic and himself appears to fall down the rabbit hole of a different type of mental illness. Ultimately, we realise that mental illness is not restricted to technical diagnoses of schizophrenia, but is actually incredibly prevalent among the post-World War I generation. The battle Nicole is fighting to stay well and happy is actually one that we are all fighting, albeit on a smaller scale.

LACK OF CHRONOLOGY AND TIMELINES

Tender is the Night stands apart from Fitzgerald's previous novels for its interesting use of timelines. Fitzgerald's prior novels usually begin with detailed backstories about the main characters and the events continue to occur in chronological order. However, this novel begins *in medias res*, in the middle of the action. This means that we are given surprisingly little information about our protagonists. Dick and Nicole are enshrouded in an air of mystery. This mystery is heightened when Violet McKisco witnesses a shocking scene in the Divers' bathroom. The revelation of what occurs in this bathroom is consciously withheld from the reader throughout the first part of the novel, building the narrative tension.

The second part of the novel goes back in time to answer these questions and offer the types of detailed character backstories that we expect from Fitzgerald. The tale of the early days of Dick and Nicole's romance makes sense of their complicated relationship throughout the first part. A reorganised chronological version of the novel was published in 1951. However, this version was widely criticised. Beginning with an explanation of Nicole's mental illness, Dick's role in her treatment, and their ultimate romance removes the mystery and tension from the remainder of the novel.

There is another effect of watching Dick's romance with Nicole follow on from his infatuation with Rosemary. Dick's love for Rosemary is primarily based on her youth, innocence and naïveté. Nicole, in contrast, is Dick's harder, older, more weathered wife. However, going back in time in the second part of the novel, we find Nicole embodying that innocence and naïveté that had seemed to define her rival. Rosemary is described as "on the last edge of childhood." (p. 12). In Part 2, we meet a version of Nicole that is extremely childlike, perhaps due in part to her mental illness. When she writes to Dick, she says childish things such as: "I have only gotten to like boys who are rather sissies. Are you a sissy?" (p. 136).

Watching Dick fall for Nicole is more tragic because of our knowledge that they ultimately fall out of love. This gives us a sense that nothing can last and everything is temporary. Nicole's position as a beacon of childlike naïveté ultimately fades and is replaced by Rosemary, and Dick's love for Nicole is ultimately replaced by his romance with Rosemary. These instances of fading are even more shocking because we watch them occur in reverse. The first time we encounter Dick and Nicole's central relationship, it is already in the process of fading. Watching the romance begin is thus tinged with the sense of disillusioned sadness that characterises much of Fitzgerald's work.

THE LOST GENERATION

Fitzgerald belonged to a literary movement called "the Lost Generation", in which a group of American writers lost faith in the American Dream. Writers such as Fitzgerald, along with Ernest Hemingway, John Dos Passos (American novelist, 1896-1970), E.E. Cummings (American poet, 1894-1962), Archibald MacLeish (American poet, 1892-1982), Hart Crane (American poet, 1899-1932) and others, moved to Paris to continue writing about the loss of American ideals. The protagonists in many of their works fought in World War I only to return to an America that had lost both its charm and its meaning for them.

The characters of Dick and Nicole Diver are said to be loosely based on Gerald and Sara Murphy, two American expatriates who frequented Fitzgerald's circle. Much like the writers of the Lost Generation, Dick and Nicole have chosen to make a life in Europe away from the traumas and disillusionment of America. They spend the majority of their time in Switzerland and in the French Riviera, an area they claim the credit for popularising. Unlike Fitzgerald's earlier novels, *Tender is the Night* occurs almost entirely outside America, likely due to the fact that Fitzgerald had been living in Paris when it was written.

In *Tender is the Night*, America represents a place where Nicole was sexually abused by her father and where Dick returns to mourn the death of his father. Although it represents the heritage of our characters, it is a place of painful and negative memories. When Dick returns to live in America at the end of the novel, it is a moment of failure. It is a moment when neither his career nor his marriage have lived up to his expectations. His disillusioned, empty life then belongs in an America that likewise feels disillusioned and empty.

FURTHER REFLECTION

SOME QUESTIONS TO THINK ABOUT...

- To what extent is Rosemary to blame for the deterioration of Dick and Nicole's marriage? Explain your answer.
- Given that she fades to the sidelines in the second and third parts of the novel, why do you think Rosemary so central to the opening of the story?
- Is it wrong for Rosemary to pursue Dick so aggressively, knowing that he is married? Explain your answer.
- How sympathetic of a character is Nicole? How does our sympathy for her develop between the first and second parts of the novel?
- What role does Nicole's wealth play in her marriage to Dick?
- How does Dick's role as a doctor and Nicole's role as a patient complicate their marriage?
- Do you think Dick ever regrets marrying Nicole? If so, when?

- What are the factors that fuel Dick's alcoholism?
- How much of Dick and Nicole's relationship is based on Fitzgerald's own relationship with Zelda and her mental health struggles? How does our understanding of the plot's autobiographical elements complicate our reading of it?

We want to hear from you!
Leave a comment on your online library
and share your favourite books on social media!

FURTHER READING

REFERENCE EDITION

- Fitzgerald, F. S. (2000) *Tender is the Night*. London: Penguin Books Ltd.

REFERENCE STUDIES

- The Editors of Encyclopædia Britannica (2016) Gerald and Sara Murphy. *Encyclopædia Britannica*. [Online]. [Accessed 31 January 2019]. Available from: <https://www.britannica.com/biography/Gerald-Murphy-and-Sara-Murphy>

- The Editors of Encyclopædia Britannica (2017) Lost Generation: American Literature. *Encyclopædia Britannica*. [Online]. [Accessed 27 December 2018]. Available from: <https://www.britannica.com/topic/Lost-Generation>

- The Editors of Encyclopædia Britannica (2015) Tender is the Night. *Encyclopædia Britannica*. [Online]. [Accessed 31 January 2019]. Available from: <https://www.britannica.com/topic/Tender-Is-the-Night>

- Mizener, A. (2018) F. Scott Fitzgerald: American Writer. *Encyclopædia Britannica*. [Online]. [Accessed 27 December 2018]. Available from: <https://www.britannica.com/biography/F-Scott-Fitzgerald>

- Zelazko, A. (2018) Zelda Fitzgerald: American Writer and Artist. *Encyclopædia Britannica*. [Online]. [Accessed 31 January 2019]. Available from: <https://www.britannica.com/biography/Zelda-Fitzgerald>

ADDITIONAL SOURCES

- Bruccoli, M. (1981) *Some Sort of Epic Grandeur: The Life of F. Scott Fitzgerald*. Columbia: University of South Carolina Press.

- Bruccoli, M. and Baughman, J. S. (2004) *Conversations with F. Scott Fitzgerald*. Jackson: University Press of Mississippi.

- Curnutt, K. (2004) *A Historical Guide to F. Scott Fitzgerald*. New York: Oxford University Press.

- Mizener, A. (1951) *The Far Side of Paradise*. Boston: Houghton Mifflin.

- Prigozy, R. (2002) *The Cambridge Companion to F. Scott Fitzgerald*. Cambridge: Cambridge University Press.

ADAPTATIONS

- *Tender is the Night*. (1962) [Film]. Henry King. Dir. USA: Twentieth Century Fox.

- *Tender is the Night*. (1985) [Mini-series]. Robert Knights. Dir. United Kingdom: British Broadcasting Corporation.

MORE FROM BRIGHTSUMMARIES.COM

- Reading guide - *The Beautiful and Damned* by F. Scott Fitzgerald.

- Reading guide – *The Great Gatsby* by F. Scott Fitzgerald.

- Reading guide – *The Last Tycoon* by F. Scott Fitzgerald.

- Reading guide – *This Side of Paradise* by F. Scott Fitzgerald.

www.brightsummaries.com

Ebook EAN: 9782808017824

Paperback EAN: 9782808017831

Legal Deposit: D/2019/12603/58

Cover: © Primento

Digital conception by Primento, the digital partner of
publishers.